SUGGESTIONS FOR GROUP LEADERS

1. THE ROOM Discourage people from sitting outside the circle - all need to be equally involved.

2. HOSPITALITY Tea or coffee on arrival and/or at the ending. Perhaps at the end too, to encourage people to stay and chat. It can be more ambitious, taking it in turns to bring a cake, etc. (but excellent, hospitality is OK!) with coffee at the end.

3. THE START If group members don't know each other well, some kind of 'icebreaker' might be helpful. For example, you might invite people to share something quite secular (where they grew up, holidays, hobbies, etc.). Place a time limit on this exercise.

4. PREPARING THE GROUP Take the group into your confidence, e.g. 'I've never done this before', or 'I've led lots of groups and each one has contained surprises'. Sharing vulnerability is designed to encourage all members to see the success of the group as their responsibility. Ask those who know that they talk easily to ration their contributions and encourage the reticent to speak at least once or twice - however briefly. Explain that there are no 'right' answers and that among friends it is fine to say things that you are not sure about - to express half-formed ideas. However, if individuals choose to say nothing, that is all right too.

5. THE MATERIAL Encourage members to read next week's chapter before the meeting. It helps enormously if each group member has their own personal copy of this booklet (so the price is reduced either when 5 or more copies are ordered or if you order online). There is no need to consider all the questions. A lively exchange of views is what matters, so be selective. You can always spread a session over two or more meetings, if the discussion is very lively!

For some questions you might start with a few minutes' silence to make jottings. Or you might ask members to talk in sub-groups of two or three, before sharing with the whole group.

6. PREPARATION Decide beforehand whether to distribute (or ask people to bring) paper, pencils, hymn books, etc. If possible, ask people in advance to read a Bible passage or lead in prayer, so that they can prepare.

7. TIMING Try to start on time and make sure you stick fairly closely to your stated finishing time.

8. USING THE CD/AUDIOTAPE Some groups will play the 14-minute piece at the beginning of the meeting. Other groups will prefer to play it at the end - or to play 7/8 minutes at the beginning and the rest halfway through the meeting. The track markers (on the CD only) will help you find any section very easily, including the Closing Reflections. Or you can ignore these markers altogether, if you prefer.

A word-by-word TRANSCRIPT booklet of the CD/audiotape is available. Many GROUP LEADERS find this helpful as they prepare. In addition, reading the transcript can help some group members feel more confident about joining in the discussion, while others may wish to go over the recorded material at leisure after the session. *(See centre pages of this booklet and/or www.yorkcourses.co.uk)*

SESSION 1

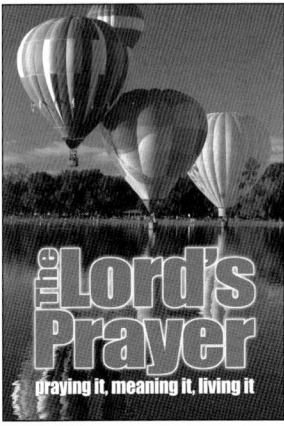

OUR FATHER

> When you pray, move your feet.
>
> *African Proverb*
>
> Prayer is not asking. It is a longing of the soul... It is better in prayer to have a heart without words than words without a heart.
>
> *Mahatma Gandhi*
>
> All prayer is audacious.
>
> *Revd Dr John Pridmore*
>
> I believe that prayer and contemplation are the most important things I do.
>
> *Bishop Stephen Cottrell*

'The Lord's Prayer'. In fact it isn't. The prayer which we call the Lord's Prayer is *our* prayer – not his.

The Lord's *own* prayer is found in John 17 and we are painfully aware that one heartfelt petition has not yet been answered: 'May they be brought to complete unity...' (verse 23).

Luke shows Jesus to be a man of prayer. He prayed at his baptism (Luke 3.21); he prayed for a whole night before choosing the twelve apostles (6.12); he prayed with thanksgiving before feeding the crowds (9.16); he prayed in anguish in the Garden of Gethsemane (22.41-44).

He prayed.

Like all Jews at that time, Jesus' disciples were men of prayer too. But his was praying with a difference. They could see this very clearly. So they made their famous request, 'Lord, teach us to pray' (Luke 11.1).

In response, Jesus gave them this prayer. He didn't give them a technique. He didn't give them a rationale. He gave them a short prayer – 34 words when translated into English. Those petitions which he uttered in Aramaic (his native language) have become the most famous and familiar words in history. Over the centuries his brief prayer has been expanded slightly into the form which we now use in our churches. And in our homes, our schools and our prisons too – though less often today than 50 years ago.

These words are a pattern for our praying – and for our living.

In this course we shall explore their significance for us today – as individuals, as churches and as communities.

Prayer has a direction

Jesus addresses this prayer to his 'Father' in Luke's Gospel; to 'our Father in heaven' in Matthew's. This is typical of Jesus' teaching. He constantly encourages his hearers to think of God as 'our heavenly Father'. God is not an impersonal 'Force'. He is Jesus' Father – and *our* Father, too. Like all good fathers, he offers unconditional love and guidance. Then he sets us free to make our own choices – dangerous, but vital if we are to flourish.

Not all prayer has an outward direction. When reviewing a recent book entitled *Buddhism and Christianity in Dialogue*, Marcus Braybrooke commented, 'There is an old story of a bishop who observed a Buddhist monk meditating. Afterwards, greeting him,

> 'Abba' expresses the heart of Jesus' relationship to God. He spoke to God as a child to its father: confidently and securely, and yet at the same time reverently and obediently.
>
> Professor Joachim Jeremias

> All monks and nuns devote their lives to prayer. From this base some gain tremendous energy, e.g. Sister Frances Dominica who founded Helen House, the world's first Children's Hospice.

the bishop said: "Isn't it wonderful that we are both people who believe in prayer?" "I am no one, praying to nobody, for nothing," was the chilling reply.'

Christian prayer is very different. The Bible does not encourage us to empty our minds and focus on 'nothingness'. Instead, it invites us to fill our minds with a multitude of images. Foremost among these is 'Our Father in heaven'.

Much is made of the experience of children with absent fathers, or abusive fathers. Rightly so, for these are harsh realities for too many children. The treasure trove of Bible images is very helpful here. We are encouraged to move from one mental picture to another, as we meditate on the Reality and Mystery which is God. If one image doesn't work for us, then we can try another – and another...

Painting pictures with words

I once led a group of young people in a search for images of God in the Bible. We scanned the Psalms and stopped when we reached over 30: Shepherd, King, Rock, Fortress... (you might go on an 'image-hunt' for yourself). The New Testament takes a similar approach. I am told that for Jesus himself there are around 100 titles and images (although I confess I haven't actually counted them!). Nothing captures this abundance more effectively than the four-line stanza from John Newton's lovely hymn, *How sweet the name of Jesus sounds*:

> Jesus! My Shepherd, Husband, Friend,
> My Prophet, Priest and King;
> My Lord, my Life, my Way, my End,
> Accept the praise I bring.

The Bible offers a cascade of word pictures. Jesus rejoiced in these riches. But for him the dominant image was of God as a tender, loving Father. Yes, God *is* concerned with the big events in world history. At the same time, the God to whom Jesus directs our gaze also cares about the smaller matters which make up our individual lives and mean so much to us. He is as involved with our cuts and bruises – and with our treats and delights – as with our careers and our marriages. The implications of this are spelt out in Peter's first letter: 'Cast all your cares upon him, for he cares for you' (1 Peter 5.7).

> Our heavenly father, if we ask him for a need, gives us these things and much more but not in an earthly way. To understand that the prayer is always answered, but in a heavenly way, is very difficult. It needs great faith and understanding.
>
> *Sister Wendy Beckett*

For some, this is wonderful good news. They have a deep personal relationship with God. They do indeed 'take it to the Lord in prayer' – whatever 'it' might be. For them, praying is living and living is praying. They talk with the

> God could not be everywhere at the same time so he invented Mothers.
> *Anon*

> In the fourteenth century Mother Julian of Norwich spoke of 'Mother Jesus' and wrote, 'As truly as God is our Father, as truly God is our Mother.'

> Elijah prayed, 'I have had enough. Take my life.' But God had other, far richer plans: plans to prosper Elijah, not to harm him; plans to give him hope and a future (Jeremiah 29.11). Praise the Lord for unanswered prayer.
> *Revd Andrew Watson*

> A lot of people come to Walsingham looking for the gift of a child, as they have been unable to conceive; and the gift has often been given.
> *Philip North, Priest Administrator of the Shrine of Our Lady of Walsingham*

Lord throughout the day – seeking guidance, offering thanks, praying for those in need...

But for other people this simply seems too good to be true. They do believe in God, but they struggle to believe that he loves each of us as individuals. As one man put it to me: 'God has a universe to run. He can't possibly be concerned about little me and my requests.'

God as Mother

In reality, of course, mothers do most of the day-to-day caring, as the Scriptures readily agree. Whether we should address God as Mother has become a hot potato with the advent of feminist theology. In fact, there is a long and honourable tradition of praying to God as our Mother. It is caught by Jesus when he compares himself to a mother hen (Luke 13.34). Centuries before that we find something similar in the prophet Isaiah (Isaiah 66.13). So Anselm (Archbishop of Canterbury 1093-1109) was not being controversial when he wrote, 'Jesus... you are gentle with us as a mother with her children.'

The key provided in the Bible is rich variety and wide choice. We are encouraged by Jesus to pray to 'our Father in heaven'. But he also directs us to the many other titles and images which are woven into the tapestry of Scripture.

Prayer has a simplicity

When church-goers are asked to list topics with which they need help, prayer is always near, or at, the top. Some churches run occasional 'practical' courses on prayer and I would encourage individuals to attend one if at all possible.

But I do wonder if we Christians sometimes mistakenly believe that there is a mystique to prayer – a key which will make all the difference. The entire lifetime of nuns and monks is built around prayer, so we might assume that they are the experts. Perhaps they are. But many of them will tell you that they struggle with the same challenges as the rest of us – issues like focusing, staying attentive, finding a way of praying that suits our personality...

In my view it is significant that Jesus didn't answer his disciples' request, 'Lord, teach us to pray', with a *method* but with a short prayer. It's as though he is saying, 'If you want to learn to pray – **pray!** Get on and **do** it!'

> Some Christians find it helpful - even life-changing - to get away for a weekend at one of the many retreat houses dotted around Britain, often in beautiful settings. www.retreats.org.uk (Tel: 0845 456 1429).

Prayer has implications

The Old Testament prophets waged war on false religion. James in the New Testament does the same. False religion is simply defined. It is religion which stops on the lips. As we pray, so must we act. Prayer is not a question of persuading God to do our will. Rather it involves opening our hearts to allow God to do his will through us. But this is a big topic and deserves a full session of its own.

QUESTIONS FOR GROUPS
BIBLE READING: Luke 11.1-13

1. 'Harold be thy name... lead us not into Thames Station.' Do you think it matters that the old words can be confusing for children? Should we use and teach the traditional and/or modern form of the prayer?

2. Describe some of the places and situations in which you have said the Lord's Prayer. What memories does this evoke for you?

3. What do you think it might have been about Jesus at prayer which prompted the disciples' request, 'Lord, teach us to pray'?

4. Describe someone who, through teaching or example, has taught you about the Christian life in general and prayer in particular.

5. Does the idea of God as 'Father' work well for you? What about the word picture of God as 'Mother'? Which other images of God and Jesus are important for you when facing life's ups and downs? Why? (See John Newton's hymn on page 3.)

6. In contrast to Muslims and Jews, many Christians (especially British Christians?) are embarrassed about praying. But you are among friends! Share with group members your own approach to praying and difficulties/joys you have with prayer. Invite others to comment.

7. If someone asked you to teach them how to pray, how would you set about it? Would the Lord's Prayer feature in your guidance? If so, why and how?

8. *Read Matthew 7.7-12* and the box from Walsingham (page 4). Share your experiences (both positive and negative) of 'answers to prayer'.

9. *Read James 1.22-27.* 'As we pray so must we live.' Prayer and worship have implications for life. Reflect on what these might be for you in the coming week - and the coming year.

10. If prayer and action are linked so closely, can you see 'the point' of purely contemplative religious orders? (See box on page 3.)

11. *Read 1 Peter 5.7.* Do you talk to the Lord through the day - or do you keep prayer for special times and/or big issues? What do you feel about the man who thought that God can't be concerned with the details of our lives (page 4)?

12. Raise any points from the course booklet or CD/audiotape which haven't been covered in your discussion, but which you find interesting.

You might wish to end each group meeting by keeping silence before saying the Lord's Prayer together.

SESSION 2

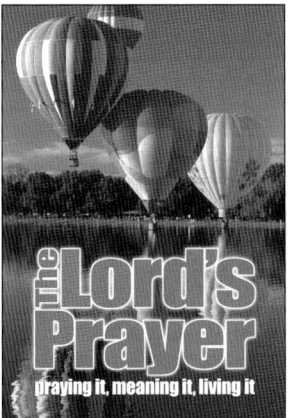

THY WILL BE DONE

The Khouds of North India have a prayer which reads, 'Lord we don't know what is good for us. You know what it is. For it we pray.'

Canon John Cockerton

The function of prayer is not to influence God, but rather to change the nature of the one who prays.

Søren Kierkegaard

The kingdom of God is not a place we arrive at, but the pole we measure from. It gives direction to our wanderings and our ways.

Canon Dr Alan Billings

'Thy will be done'. Four familiar words. Words which we sometimes utter before our minds are in gear. But if our minds – and our wills – are engaged, and we see them for what they are, they become four very explosive words. These words spell danger, for God might call our bluff.

'Nevertheless, your will, not mine, be done' (Mark 14.36). When Jesus uttered those words in the Garden of Gethsemane, he wasn't bluffing. And God his Father took them at face value. Without that short phrase, spoken by Jesus out of anguish and with total sincerity, there would be no cross – and no Easter either.

But we are running ahead of ourselves. Jesus had less dramatic things in mind when he first taught his disciples to pray, 'Thy will be done'.

Less dramatic does not mean unimportant. So central was this theme to his teaching that Jesus put the same notion in three different ways in his pattern prayer. 'Thy Kingdom come', 'hallowed be Thy name' and 'Thy will be done' all amount to much the same thing.

'Thy Kingdom come' is a vital summary of Jesus' teaching – and of his life. But in the Gospels the Kingdom of God isn't a place. The phrase refers to God's kingly rule – his lordship in our world and in our lives. So 'Thy Kingdom come' is another way of praying 'Thy will be done'.

Clear and obvious

Much of the time, God's will for us is clear. Jesus calls us to be alert to the needs of our neighbours, generous in our estimate of others, quick to forgive. He calls us to accept life as a gift from God, to take any knocks along the way as part of its 'rich tapestry', and to live in a manner which commends our faith to those around us. This is the way of life to which we pledge ourselves, every time we pray the Lord's Prayer.

This can be tremendously powerful. What was it that enabled the gospel to take root and flourish in the hostile soil of the Roman Empire? It was the sheer attractiveness of their joy in living, peace in adversity and care for others shown by the early Christians. The Graeco-Roman world was a macho world. Gentleness, tenderness and forgiveness were despised by many. Yet, in the end, these values overcame brutality and revenge.

In the fourth century, the anti-Christian Emperor Julian came to the throne. He accused the Christians of atheism, because they believed in one invisible God – and a God who could not be seen or touched was no

> Atheism [i.e. Christian faith] has been specially advanced through the loving service rendered to strangers and through their care for the burial of the dead... the godless Galileans [a wonderful term for the early Christians!] care not only for their own poor but for ours as well.
>
> *Emperor Julian (331-363)*

God at all! Julian was determined to reinstate the pagan gods. He failed, and was honest enough to say why (see box).

Through a glass darkly

Sometimes day-to-day living is complicated and we find ourselves in situations which are morally ambiguous. Should I drop everything when the old lady down the road rings in apparent distress? Well of course I should. But what if that means cancelling a meeting which has involved others in travel? What should I do then? All of us face tensions of this kind from time to time.

And of course we all have to make big personal decisions – where to live, which job, whether to marry... Sometimes these things fall into place easily, but they can cause anxiety and stress.

In America – and to a lesser extent in the UK – the WWJD movement has become popular. Lapel badges and car stickers ask the same question: *What Would Jesus Do?* Yes, of course it's simplistic. It's easy to mock. But for many it's an honest, heartfelt attempt to work through a maze of moral ambiguities.

> The word 'lord' means 'boss'... There are many ways of defining what 'a Christian' is. The best one is this: a Christian is one who takes orders from Jesus Christ as Lord.
>
> *Dean David L Edwards*

Bigger questions

Moral ambiguity applies on a wider canvas, too. We pray 'Thy will be done' in the public arena, as well as in our personal lives and relationships. But what *is* God's will?

For instance, should we encourage stem cell research, in order to lessen human suffering? Or might this lead to Aldous Huxley's nightmare of a Brave New World?

Should we legalise euthanasia or assisted suicide? When we hear people *in extremis* asking to be 'released' (usually on our TV screens but just occasionally face to face), we feel the emotional strength of their arguments. But is there a slippery slope waiting for us? Would such legislation perhaps put pressure on old people not to be 'a burden' on their families?

Just what does 'Thy will be done' mean in practical terms in our complex twenty-first century?

> A real Christian is not only a good and well-intentioned person but a man or woman for whom Jesus Christ is ultimately decisive; for whom Jesus – not Caesar, not another god, not money, sex, power or pleasure – is Lord.
>
> *Professor Hans Küng*

Temptation

Even if God's will for us is clear, there still remains the small matter of actually *doing* it. 'Lead us not into temptation' is an inescapable part of this most famous prayer. But what an odd phrase it is. Why on earth – or

> The idea of the kingdom coming was very near the centre of Jesus' teaching. And the kingdom is not a place or a system – it's just a state of affairs when God really is acknowledged to be directing and giving meaning to everything. It's the kingship of God, if you like.
>
> *Archbishop Rowan Williams*

in heaven – would God do that? But he famously did on at least one occasion. It was an experience which burned itself into Jesus' mind and heart.

God led Jesus into the wilderness just before his public ministry began. That period of 40 days was a preparation for his ministry – and for his crucifixion. Long hours of solitude; an inhospitable desert; extremes of heat and cold; desperate hunger – and rather low-key temptations. None of them involved what we regard as the really *big* sins. We've had plenty of those over the past few decades: mass murder; torture; genocide; swindles on a vast scale, with subsequent poverty for pensioners...

All these mega-sins begin in the mind and in the heart. That's where Jesus' battle raged. His temptations were about *compromise*. The devil urged him to take the easy road – the one that leads to spiritual destruction. Instead, he chose the rugged road. That road would lead to physical destruction for him – and life for us. It was a tough choice, which didn't come easily to Jesus.

This time of mental turmoil in the wilderness set the pattern for his ministry. He knew from the beginning that 'the Son of Man came not to be served, but to serve, and to give his life as a ransom for many' (Mark 10.45).

What about us?

On a much smaller canvas, this temptation to compromise is our temptation too. Few of us are tempted to violence (for one thing, we're too weak and too frightened) or to large-scale cheating (in any case, we don't have the wherewithal). But we are frequently tempted to compromise – to take the easy road; to pamper ourselves; to look out for Number One.

> Thy will be done ... this is the risky, crazy prayer of submission and ... conversion. It is the way we sign on, in our turn, for the work of the kingdom.
>
> *Bishop Tom Wright*

Many well-meaning, sometimes surprising, voices encourage us down that road – telling us that we need to take care of ourselves. Even the Archbishops of Canterbury and York have put their stamp of approval on a booklet for Lent which has on its front cover, 'Be generous to yourself'. Yes, we know what they mean but... The New Testament often uses strikingly different language (Colossians 3.1-5). It bids us deny ourselves, take up our cross, lose ourselves...

Give me low standards and I'll hit them every time. So perhaps we *do* need to ask, 'What would Jesus do?'

QUESTIONS FOR GROUPS
BIBLE READING: Matthew 12.46-50

1. Re-read the section *Through a glass darkly* (page 8). Describe one or two personal situations when you found it difficult to discern the right way forward. This can be run-of-the-mill, like my experience with an elderly neighbour. Or you might focus on one of life's big decisions.

2. *Discerning* God's will is one thing; *doing* God's will is something else. If you are willing, describe to your group a time when you faced a temptation to compromise – or any other temptation. Invite group members to share insights arising from your dilemma – and from their own experiences.

3. Re-read the first paragraph in the section *Clear and obvious* (page 7). Can you describe an individual or church which fits this description? What about your own local church? How can you get closer to this blueprint?

4. Do you think the WWJD approach could be helpful for you? Are you willing to try it for a week or two? If so, what do you anticipate?

5. 'Thy will be done' applies to society as well as individuals. Read the box about abortion (below). Then draw up a short list of other morally ambiguous dilemmas confronting Church and Society, e.g. assisted suicide. Select one for further discussion.

6. *Read Luke 4.1-13.* As you reflect on Jesus' temptations in the wilderness, select one aspect which you find inspiring or moving and/or one which you find intriguing or even confusing. Share insights.

7. *Read Hebrews 4.14-16.* What does this mean for our understanding of Jesus and for our understanding of temptation and sin?

8. *Read Mark 8.34-37.* Re-read the paragraph entitled 'What about us?' (page 9). Are you on the side of the Archbishops? Or do you think I am right? Why?

9. *Read Matthew 13.31-35 and 44-46.* What light do these brief parables of the Kingdom (or 'Rule') of God throw on the phrases, 'Thy Kingdom come' and 'Thy will be done' – and the modern term 'Kingdom values'? (You might find it helpful to read the words of David L Edwards and Hans Küng in the boxes on page 8.)

10. Raise any points from the course booklet or CD/audiotape which haven't been covered in your discussion but which you find interesting.

In August 2007 *Amnesty International* fell out with the Roman Catholic Church over abortion. This was very painful, for *Amnesty* was founded by a Catholic and thousands of Catholics support it. *Amnesty* is particularly concerned for rape victims. Supporters of their position argue that we can never prevent abortion, and if we try to do so completely, 'backstreet abortions' will flourish. To the Catholic Church, abortion is baby murder by another name. (*Note:* in Britain there are some 600 legal abortions carried out each day.)

SESSION 3

OUR DAILY BREAD

Never has our daily bread had so much prominence. Publishers make a fortune from books extolling the virtue of this diet or that. TV schedules are full of programmes produced in kitchens great and small. Headlines declare that fashion models are leading young girls astray – too thin – while poor diets are leading young boys astray – too fat.

These are developments I couldn't have imagined when I grew up in those far-off days of rationing during and after World War II. My parents 'dug for victory' and – despite those ration books – it seems that we lived in a golden age with an almost perfect diet!

Precarious times

'Give us this day our daily bread'. Let's revisit those days 2,000 years ago, when this short petition was first offered.

Jesus and his generation depended on the labours of farmers and fishermen. And no doubt most people grew what they could around their living space. With no refrigeration and little storage, famine was a constant fear. All that was needed for anguish and widespread suffering – even death – was a lengthy drought, a single blight or an unwelcome visit from locusts. This is much better understood by the billions in today's world who still live without refrigeration – or even electricity.

This simple request for daily bread, given to his first disciples by Jesus, continues to address life and death issues for millions in the modern world. Many of these are young, for the developing world is teeming with children. As a boy, John Sentamu, now Archbishop of York, was asked by his father to say Grace. They lived in Uganda and food was short. He was rebuked by his father when he told the Lord that he would be more grateful if there was more food for supper!

Sharing

To pray for our own daily bread so soon after saying 'Thy will be done' has implications. The thrust of these implications is clear enough. But their application is less obvious.

'Eat up your greens,' urged my mother. 'Think about all the people who don't have anything to eat.' Well, I would gladly have packed up my cabbage into a parcel and sent it off first class (except that first and second class post weren't invented until much later!). The problem persists. Just *how* can I share my food with a hungry African family? There are ways, of course, but

---

Our planet needs to produce more food over the coming 50 years than it did during the last 10,000 years combined. *Conclusion of a Scientific Convention on soil conservation in August 2007*

Help the Aged reports (June 2007) that persistent poverty still exists among older people in the UK: 11 per cent are living in severe poverty, and 21 per cent are below the median line of earnings. The average weekly disposable income is £138 for single pensioners.

> Worldwide movement against globalisation
>
> *Slogan on a placard protesting against G8 summit leaders*

> Angela Murray of *Toybox* (a Christian charity) works with street children. In November 2006 she reported that, according to the United Nations, an estimated 100 million children live on the streets – 40 million of them in Latin America.

> 2.4 billion people have no proper sanitation... every 15 seconds a child dies from a water-related disease.

> Did you know...?
> - The first people believed to have grown cocoa beans were the Olmec Indians, around 1500 BC.
> - The English Quaker Joseph Fry created the first chocolate bar in 1847.
> - In 2006 Britons spent £4.3bn on chocolate.

they are not altogether obvious and straightforward. This doesn't excuse me, though it does sometimes confuse me.

Warnings about global warming* have made this even more complicated. We are urged to 'buy local' but this alarms thousands of small-scale farmers in Kenya whose whole way of life now depends upon supermarkets flying in their produce.

Our consuming society

Few Christians in the West feel any real urgency to pray for 'our daily bread'. We take bread on the table for granted. And cake too. Personally, I refuse to feel guilty about this. I didn't ask to be born of British parents into an austere, though now affluent, society. Rather than feel guilty, I give thanks for a planet teeming with abundance, and pray and work (very inadequately) for a more just and compassionate world. And I try to be moderate in my lifestyle (not difficult, for I am naturally stingy!).

This surely is more positive than 'beating myself up' because of circumstances which I can't change, i.e. my 'accident' of birth. But to some readers this will seem disastrously complacent. For them, consumerism – and perhaps globalisation, too – are giants to be slain.

Physical can be spiritual

Archbishop William Temple asserted that Christianity is the most *material* of all the great world religions. Christian faith is not just about 'the life of the spirit'. It is strongly physical – sacramental – too. It embraces *every* aspect of life. Jesus made this clear when he put this petition about daily bread in the middle of his pattern prayer.

We 'do not live by bread alone'. By quoting that phrase from the Old Testament (Deuteronomy 8.3) when he is tempted, Jesus makes clear that we need to nourish our spirits on the Word of God. But the Bible carries a tough and tangy 'physical' faith. Jesus fed 5,000 then 4,000. He healed people's bodies. On the cross he cried out, 'I thirst' (John 19.28). And he gave us the Sacraments – bread, wine, water – which carry vital material messages about God's love, mercy and grace.

---

*Climate Change and Christian Faith – a CD featuring leading scientist Sir John Houghton CBE, FRS is available from York Courses (see centre pages of this booklet).

Courses for groups
Prices held until 1st September 2008

THE LORD'S PRAYER
praying it, meaning it, living it

with **Canon Margaret Sentamu, Bishop Kenneth Stevenson, Dr David Wilkinson.** Closing Reflections by **Dr Elaine Storkey.** Introduced by **Dr David Hope**

FIVE SESSIONS: *Our Father; Thy will be done; Our daily bread; As we forgive; In heaven*

In the Lord's Prayer Jesus gives us a pattern for living as his disciples. This famous prayer also raises vital questions for today's world in which 'daily bread' is uncertain for billions and a refusal to 'forgive those who trespass against us' escalates violence.

CAN WE BUILD A BETTER WORLD?
learning from William Wilberforce

with **Archbishop John Sentamu, Wendy Craig, Leslie Griffiths.** Closing Reflections by **Five Poor Clares from BBC TV's The Convent.** Introduced by **Dr David Hope**

FIVE SESSIONS: *Slavery: then and now; Friendship & Prayer: then and now; Change & Struggle: then and now; The Bible: then and now; Redemption & Restitution: then and now*

We live in a divided and hurting world and with a burning question. As Christians in the 21st century how can we – together with others of good will – build a better world? Important material for important questions.

WHERE IS GOD...?

with **Archbishop Rowan Williams, Patricia Routledge** CBE, **Joel Edwards, Dr Pauline Webb.** Introduced by **Dr David Hope**

FIVE SESSIONS: *Where is God…? when we … try to make sense of life? … seek happiness? … face suffering? … make decisions? … contemplate death?*

If we are to find honest answers to these 5 challenges we need to do some serious and open thinking. Where better to do this than with trusted friends in a study group around this course?

Each group needs 1 CD or audiotape, plus a course booklet for each member. In addition many groups find the transcript booklet extremely helpful.

The **COURSE BOOKLET** has five Chapters, each with questions aimed at provoking wide-ranging discussion.

The **COURSE CD** (or audio tape) consists of five Sessions of approximately 14 minutes each, in the style of a radio programme, during which each participant contributes. Canon Simon Stanley, a former BBC Producer/Presenter, chairs each of these discussion-starters.

The words as spoken on the CD/audiotape for the course are set out in the **TRANSCRIPT** – ideal for Group Leaders when preparing and for Group Members to read before or after each session.

A transcript is now available for every course.

BETTER TOGETHER?

with **the Abbot of Ampleforth, John Bell, Nicky Gumbel, Jane Williams.** Introduced by **Dr David Hope**

FIVE SESSIONS: *Family Relationships; Church Relationships; Relating to Strangers; Broken Relationships; Our Relationship with God*

This course is about relationships – in the church and within family and society; building strong relationships and coping with broken ones. *Better Together?* looks frankly at how the Christian perspective may differ from that of society at large.

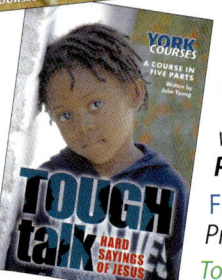

TOUGH TALK
Hard Sayings of Jesus

with **Bishop Tom Wright, Steve Chalke, Fr Gerard Hughes SJ, Professor Frances Young.** Introduced by **Dr David Hope**

FIVE SESSIONS: *Shrinking and Growing; Giving and Using; Praying and Forgiving; Loving and Telling; Trusting and Entering*

Tough Talk looks at many of the hard sayings of Jesus in the Bible and faces them squarely. His uncomfortable words need to be faced if we are to allow the full impact of the gospel on our lives. *Tough Talk* is not for the faint-hearted.

NEW WORLD, OLD FAITH

with **Archbishop Rowan Williams, David Coffey, Joel Edwards, Revd Dr John Polkinghorne** KBE FRS, **Dr Pauline Webb.** Introduced by **Dr David Hope**

FIVE SESSIONS: *Brave New World?; Environment and Ethics; Church and Family in Crisis?; One World – Many Faiths; Spirituality and Superstition*

New World, Old Faith looks at how Christian faith continues to shed light on a range of issues in our changing world, including change itself. This course helps us make sense of our faith in God in today's world.

IN THE WILDERNESS

with **Cardinal Cormac Murphy-O'Connor, Archbishop David Hope, Revd Dr Rob Frost, Roy Jenkins, Dr Elaine Storkey**

FIVE SESSIONS: *Jesus, Satan and the Angels; The Wilderness Today; The Church in the Wilderness; Prayer, Meditation and Scripture; Solitude, Friendship and Fellowship*

Like Jesus, we all have wilderness experiences. What are we to make of these challenges and how are we to meet them? *In the Wilderness* explores these issues for our world, for the church, and at a personal level.

> **"** I think that these courses are some of the best things that the Church of England has produced over the years **"**
> Dr David Hope

PRICES FOR THESE 11 COURSES

BOOKLET:	£3.50	(*£2.75* each for 5 or more)
AUDIOTAPE:	£8.95	(*£6.95* each for 5 or more)
CD:	£10.95	(*£8.95* each for **2** or more)
TRANSCRIPT:	£4.95	(*£2.95* each for **2** or more)

Free packing and 2nd class postage within the UK

FAITH IN THE FIRE NOW AVAILABLE ON CD
with **Archbishop David Hope, Rabbi Lionel Blue, Steve Chalke, Revd Dr Leslie Griffiths, Ann Widdecombe** MP

FIVE SESSIONS: *Faith facing Facts; Faith facing Doubt; Faith facing Disaster; Faith fuelling Prayer; Faith fuelling Action*

When things are going well our faith may remain untroubled, but what if doubt or disaster strike? Those who struggle with faith will find they are not alone.

JESUS REDISCOVERED NOW AVAILABLE ON CD
with **Paul Boateng** MP**, Dr Lavinia Byrne, Joel Edwards, Bishop Tom Wright, Archbishop David Hope**

FIVE SESSIONS: *Jesus' Life and Teaching; Following Jesus; Jesus: Saviour of the World; Jesus is Lord; Jesus and the Church*

Jesus Rediscovered is truly about *re*-discovering who Jesus was, what he taught, and what that means for his followers today. Several believers share what Jesus means to them.

LIVE YOUR FAITH NOW AVAILABLE ON CD
with **Revd Dr Donald English, Lord Tonypandy, Fiona & Roy Castle**

SIX SESSIONS: *The Key - Jesus; Prayer; The Community - The Church; The Dynamic - The Holy Spirit; The Bible; The Outcome - Service & Witness*

Christianity isn't just about what we believe: it's about how we live. A course suitable for everyone; particularly good for enquirers and those in the early stages of their faith.

GREAT EVENTS, DEEP MEANINGS NOW AVAILABLE ON CD
with **Revd Dr John Polkinghorne** KBE FRS**, Gordon Wilson, David Konstant** - RC Bishop of Leeds**; Fiona Castle, Dame Cicely Saunders, Archbishop David Hope**

SIX SESSIONS: *Christmas; Ash Wednesday; Palm Sunday; Good Friday; Easter; Pentecost*

Explains clearly what the feasts and fasts are about and challenges us to respond spiritually and practically. There are even a couple of quizzes to get stuck into!

2 ADDITIONAL COURSES
– comprising photocopyable notes, audiotape & transcript

ATTENDING, EXPLORING, ENGAGING
with **Archbishop David Hope, Steve Chalke, Fr Gerard Hughes SJ, Professor Frances Young**

FIVE SESSIONS: *Attending to God; Attending to One Another; Exploring Our Faith; Engaging with the World in Service; Engaging with the World in Evangelism*

THE TEACHING OF JESUS
with **Steve Chalke, Professor James Dunn, Dr Pauline Webb, Archbishop David Hope**

FIVE SESSIONS: *Forgiveness; God; Money; Heaven and Hell; On Being Human*

AUDIOTAPE: £8.95 (£6.95 each for 5 or more) **PHOTOCOPYABLE NOTES: £2.50**
TRANSCRIPT: £4.95 (£2.95 each for 2 or more)

For individual listening

A convinced Christian, Sir John Houghton CBE, FRS was Professor of Atmospheric Physics at Oxford University. He is a world expert on global warming, its implications and remedies. In a wide-ranging conversation with Canon John Young, Sir John talks on this **CD** about "Why I believe in Climate Change" and "Why I believe in Jesus Christ". **£7.50**

TOPIC TAPES
STRUGGLING/COPING

TAPE 1: **£5.00**
Living with **depression;** Living with **panic attacks**
TAPE 2: **£5.00** (Set of 2 tapes **£8.50**)
Living with **cancer;** Living with **bereavement**
Four personal conversations

SCIENCE AND CHRISTIAN FAITH £5.00
An in-depth discussion with the **Revd Dr John Polkinghorne** KBE FRS, former Professor of Mathematical Physics at Cambridge University

EVANGELISM TODAY £5.00
with contributions by **Canon Robin Gamble**, the **Revd Brian Hoare, Bishop Gavin Reid** and **Canon Robert Warren**

FINDING FAITH £1.95
is a 20-minute audiotape, designed for enquirers and church members. Four brief stories by people, including **Archbishop David Hope**, who have found faith.
Inexpensive! Designed as a 'give away'

PRAYER £3.50
SIDE 1: **Archbishop David Hope** on *Prayer*
SIDE 2: Four Christians on praying … *for healing; in danger; in tongues; with perseverance*
This tape accompanies the booklet
The Archbishop's School of Prayer
(see details above)

Books and booklets

ARCHBISHOP'S SCHOOL SERIES
7 BOOKLETS COMMISSIONED BY Dr DAVID HOPE – Prayer; Bible Reading; Evangelism; The Sacraments; Christianity and Science; Healing and Wholeness; Life After Death.

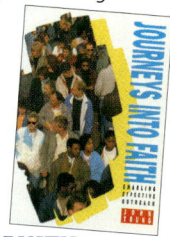

Authors include John Polkinghorne & David Winter
95p each
Special offer: You may order a complete set of all seven booklets for only £5

BOOKS BY JOHN YOUNG
(author of the course booklets)
John has work in several languages including Chinese, Korean and Russian

THE CASE AGAINST CHRIST £7.99

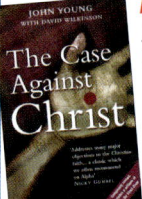

Fully revised in 2006
John Young acts as Counsel for the Defence in the Case against Christ.
"A classic" *Nicky Gumbel*
"John Young has a great gift for communicating profound ideas simply and readably"
Archbishop John Habgood

JOURNEYS INTO FAITH
A4 workbook for groups to encourage effective outreach
Was **£7.99** now **£2.50**
Published by *Churches Together in England* and *The Bible Society*

TEACH YOURSELF CHRISTIANITY £8.99
An introduction to Christianity as a living faith.

"not only informs, it excites"
Dr David Hope
"… this important book"
Bishop James Jones
"An amazing compilation. Brilliant!"
Dr Peter Brierley
Published by *Hodder & Stoughton*

York Courses · PO Box 343 · York YO19 5YB
Tel: 01904 466516 · Fax: 01904 630577 · email: courses@yorkcourses.co.uk
Visit www.yorkcourses.co.uk for the latest special offers and discounts plus secure online ordering
Payment with order please. Cheques: York Courses
FREE PACKING AND 2nd CLASS POSTAGE IN THE UK

> The Asian Christian D T Niles defined evangelism as 'one beggar showing another beggar where he found bread'.

> 'Twas God the word that spake it, He took the Bread and brake it; And what the word did make it; That I believe, and take it.
>
> *Queen Elizabeth I*

> When Jesus came into the world, he loved it so much that he gave his life for it. And what did he do? He made himself the Bread of Life. He became small, fragile, and defenceless for us.
>
> *Mother Teresa*

But William Temple had something even deeper in mind. He was referring to the Incarnation, when 'the Word became flesh and dwelt among us, full of grace and truth' (John 1.14). Despite all those cleaned-up Christmas cards (which I love), we know that in reality there was blood and pain and afterbirth and exhausting risk for Mary, Joseph and their fragile baby. 'He who was in the form of God', writes St Paul, 'humbled himself...' (Philippians 2.6-8).

Throughout his ministry Jesus was concerned with food and drink, with money and physical health. And according to the New Testament, our bodies are temples – temples of God's Spirit. That, urges the apostle, has serious implications for the way in which we live and interact with others (1 Corinthians 3.16,17).

'Spiritually-minded' people have often struggled with this 'physicality'. In the early Church there was a group called Docetists. That term comes from the Greek word *dokeo* which means 'I seem'. The notion that Jesus had a real body was difficult – and probably distasteful – for Docetists. Some even believed that Jesus escaped crucifixion, arguing that Judas or Simon of Cyrene changed places with him.

This false spirituality found expression in the suspicion of sex and exaltation of celibacy which marked so many Christian centuries. Some would argue that it is this mindset which dominates current debate on homosexuality. Others maintain that the core issue in this debate is not sex itself, but the authority and interpretation of the Bible in the life of the Church and the individual believer.

That particular argument rumbles on... over to you!

Note: Enjoy this little story now – and revisit it when tackling Session 5

A man dies and St Peter meets him at the pearly gates: "Tell me all the good things you've done. I'll give you points for each item, depending on how good it was. If you reach 100 points, you get into heaven."

"Well," the man says, confidently, "I attended church all my life and supported its ministry with my money and my time." "That's wonderful," says St Peter, "that's certainly worth one point."

A bit shaken, the man goes on. "One point? Golly. How about this: I started a soup kitchen in my town and worked in a shelter for homeless people." "Terrific!" says St Peter, "Two points for that."

"TWO POINTS!!" the man cries, "At this rate the only way I get into heaven is by the grace of God!" "Wonderful – you've hit the jackpot!" says St Peter. "Come on in!"

QUESTIONS FOR GROUPS

BIBLE READING: John 6.28-35

1. A friend offers to cook your favourite meal to celebrate your birthday. What would you choose? And which two single items of food would you name as favourites? (Porridge and toast for me – I'm a morning person!)

2. From there you might embark on a wide-ranging discussion of food in our society – from obesity to anorexia; from packaging to buying local produce.

3. What changes in attitudes to food and drink have you observed in your lifetime?

4. Jews, Muslims and other faith communities have clear food laws and guidelines. Christians don't have these – but is there a 'Christian approach' to food?

5. One-third of the world has easy access to limitless supplies of food, while the other two-thirds would be astonished at the huge wastage of food in our society. Are we powerless to remedy this? Practical suggestions please.

6. Read the paragraph on Kenyan farmers (top of page 12). What is the right way forward, in your view?

7. We do not 'live by bread alone'. What do you understand by this famous quotation from the Old Testament, used by Jesus during his temptations in the wilderness?

8. The Sacraments* can be defined as 'outward and visible signs of inward and spiritual grace'. They show how spiritual and physical realities overlap and intersect. What goes on in your head and heart when you attend a Baptism and/or take part in Holy Communion?

9. Re-read the short section *Our consuming society* on page 12. Am I being callous – or realistic? If you disagree with me, what would you say to put me on the right path?

10. When thinking about Jesus, most of us swing between stressing his divinity (and perhaps losing sight of him as a real man) and thinking of him as human (and perhaps failing to glimpse his true majesty). Share your own mental picture of Jesus and how he relates to your life.

11. *Read 1 Corinthians 3.16-17 and 1 Peter 2.4-5; 9-10.* What does it mean in practical terms to be a 'temple of God's spirit'?

12. Re-read the final two paragraphs in this session (page 13). Do you think today's Church is preoccupied with sex – or is that a rumour kept alive by the media? In either case what can, and what should, we do about it – if anything?

13. You might also want to discuss whether the Church should ordain practising homosexuals (against the current rules for most denominations) and/or ordain those with a homosexual orientation who remain celibate (which is within the rules).

14. *Read Matthew 10.42.* Some materials have immense significance in the Bible. In closing, place water, bread and wine on a table. Reflect on these in silence and then ask group members to share the thoughts which went through their minds.

---

*The Archbishop's School of the Sacraments by Simon Stanley develops this theme (see centre pages).

*Give us this day our daily bread
(Matthew 6.11)*

SESSION 4

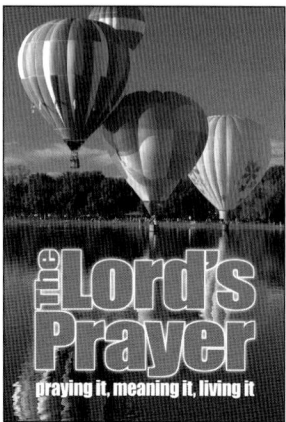

AS WE FORGIVE

Preachers are encouraged to prepare with the Bible on one side of the desk and a newspaper on the other. In other words, the ancient wisdom of the Scriptures needs to be applied in today's world.

Sometimes it is difficult to bridge the centuries between the ancient and modern worlds. As L P Hartley famously put it, 'The past is a foreign country; they do things differently there.' But some topics from our ancient Scriptures speak to our world with freshness and little need for interpretation. Forgiveness is an obvious – and extremely important – example. This topic is often in today's news, and it was central to the teaching of Jesus.

Two remarkable examples

Abigail Witchalls, a devout Catholic, was out walking with her young son in April 2005 when she was stabbed in the neck. Abigail's husband, Benoit, described her plight: 'It may well be that she's going to be paralysed from the neck down for life but people live wonderful lives paralysed from the neck down.' Asked if he could appreciate that some people would find it remarkable that he felt no anger, Benoit said: 'Maybe it will come... Obviously whoever did it needs help and it would be absolutely tragic if this was to happen again.' Subsequently, Abigail's family took her on a pilgrimage to Lourdes.

* * *

During an outdoor Remembrance Day Service in Enniskillen in 1987, a terrorist bomb killed and maimed several worshippers. One of those murdered was Marie Wilson, who had been standing next to her father. Gordon described his final conversation with his daughter and his feelings toward her killers: 'She held my hand tightly, and gripped me as hard as she could. She said, "Daddy, I love you very much." Those were her exact words to me, and those were the last words I ever heard her say.' He continued, 'But I bear no ill will. I bear no grudge. Dirty sort of talk is not going to bring her back to life. She was a great wee lassie. She loved her profession [nursing]. She was a pet. She's dead. She's in heaven and we shall meet again. I will pray for these men tonight and every night.'

The world found those words inspiring and 'the wee draper from the wee town' found himself in the spotlight. He was commended by the Queen in her Christmas Day broadcast. Although a resident of Northern Ireland, in 1993 Gordon Wilson was invited to become a Senator in the Parliament of the Republic of Ireland.

> After the war... I had a teacher who called me, 'Little Jap boy'. That stung. But my parents taught me that being bitter only pickles the one that stews in the brine. Good advice... Once you realize that those who hurt you also hurt themselves, it is easier to forgive them. And that's liberating.
>
> *George Takei, actor*

When Gordon visited York I had the great privilege of interviewing him in York's largest theatre. Hundreds of people wanted to see and hear this ordinary man who had found such extraordinary personal depths. It became clear to me that the world desperately needs public acts of forgiveness of this kind, if the cycle of violence in so many conflicts is to be broken. Sadly, Gordon did not live to see the 'impossible' sight of Ian Paisley and Gerry Adams sitting side by side in March 2007, nor to celebrate the power-sharing devolved government established at Stormont shortly after.

Admiration for Gordon Wilson was not universal, however. One woman wrote asking when he was going to stop dancing on his daughter's grave.

Too difficult?

Understandably, not everyone can find the ability to forgive so readily. My own trials have been totally insignificant compared with his. But like all adults and most children, I have been stung by unkind words and made indignant by unjust actions. When this happens I have to sit on my immediate response very firmly. It is wise to count to ten if I don't want to live with remorse and shame. Forgiveness usually takes time. And it is salutary to reflect on the hurts I have inflicted on others over the years.

Some people who have been badly hurt admit that they find forgiveness extremely difficult – even impossible. They can't, and possibly don't want to, find it within themselves to take the road travelled by Abigail and Benoit Witchalls and Gordon Wilson. Julie Nicholson is a prominent and very honest example of this. Julie's daughter, Jenny, was tragically killed in the 7/7 terrorist attacks on London. She was on the Circle Line train which was targeted by a suicide bomber on 7 July 2005.

In 2006 Julie made headlines when she gave up her job as a parish priest following the death of her daughter. This wasn't because she had lost her faith. Rather, it was because of her profound inner struggle with forgiveness. Julie Nicholson (now a theatre director) does, in fact, continue to exercise her ministry within the Church. But she felt she couldn't lead her congregation week by week in those demanding words from the Lord's Prayer, 'Forgive us our trespasses, as we forgive those who trespass against us.'

Julie recalled a terrible episode in Dostoevsky's *The Brothers Karamazov*. In this great novel, Dostoevsky,

---

God will forgive.
It's his job.
Voltaire, when nearing death

Let him who seeks revenge remember to dig two graves.
Ancient Chinese proverb

You can't keep blaming yourself. Just blame yourself once, then move on.
Homer Simpson

But because, as it is written, 'for all of us make many mistakes', let the feeling of mercy be first aroused and the faults of others against us be forgotten; that we may not violate by any love of revenge that most holy command, to which we bind ourselves in the Lord's Prayer, when we say: 'forgive us our sins as we forgive those who sin against us'.
*Leo the Great
(Pope from 440-61)*

> There were times when I felt a lot of anger and rage, and yet there was something in me that was saying that if I followed those feelings through I would end up being a victim for ever. I wanted to find a way so that I wasn't going to lose my humanity through this appalling trauma.
>
> *Jo, whose father Sir Anthony Berry was killed in the Brighton Bombing in October 1984*

himself a radical Christian, wrote about a sadistic landowner who threw a serf's child to his dogs. Ivan Karamazov speaks with great passion, 'I don't want the child's mother to embrace the torturer... The sufferings of her tortured child she has no right to forgive.'

Anyone who has not been through such dark experiences would be unwise to make judgements. Did not Jesus also say, 'Judge not, lest ye be judged' (Matthew 7.1)? But I will offer this comment. I wonder if Julie Nicholson is setting the bar too high? Jesus was, I believe, speaking about *actions* rather than *emotions*. When he declared that we must love our enemies, he was not demanding the impossible. He was not asking us to *like* them. I doubt that he felt warm thoughts towards his own executioners, even though he asked God to forgive them.

Two kinds of forgiveness

Jesus was certainly commanding his hearers not to take revenge against their tormentors. More positively, he was urging them – and us – to offer practical help to their abusers, if opportunity arose. He demands that we seek the best for them – perhaps by visiting them in prison, or giving them water to drink, or writing letters or... And he insists that we should pray for those who misuse and abuse us.

I suspect that Julie has passed all these tests.

In other words, I believe that Jesus requires *practical forgiveness* (always possible), not *emotional forgiveness* (which may take years). This is not something that we can conjure up on demand – though practical forgiveness often helps to bring about emotional forgiveness. If I am right, we can *practise* forgiveness without *feeling* forgiving.

> The bottom line... for me anyway, is not about doing what is right or worrying about what is wrong in terms of forgiveness but expressing what is real... an absence of forgiveness does not automatically equate with a desire for revenge. That is something quite different.
>
> *Revd Julie Nicholson*

Forgiveness certainly does not involve sentimental softness. When he was a vicar in Ealing, Michael Saward was clubbed unconscious and his daughter was raped. He said that he forgave their attackers but hoped they would get stiff prison sentences. Is this true forgiveness? Some might doubt that it is, while others will agree with Michael Saward that we can forgive fully while demanding justice.

'Deliver us from evil'

This phrase from the Lord's Prayer is far-reaching and it certainly applies to the corrosive effects of bitterness.

> If we take the teaching of Jesus seriously, we will not take it literally – much of the time anyway. For Jesus sets out to tease – even shock – our minds into action by using exaggeration and outrageous statements (Luke 14.26). His intention is to point us in a certain direction – to a life in which faith, hope and love reign supreme. Grasp this and you are 'not far from the Kingdom of God' (Mark 12.34).

Bitterness locks us into the past. Forgiveness – as understood in the robust form outlined above – sets us free to pick up the threads of peaceful living. It enables us to re-build our lives, however slowly.

Instant full forgiveness in the Abigail Witchalls and Gordon Wilson mould may not always be the right way forward, in my view. Our approach should take account of circumstances, personalities, relationships and the passage of time. It would be wrong to ask an abused child or beaten wife to forgive and forget. Going public or attending a course in assertiveness, to help build self-esteem, might be more appropriate – though a just outcome and forgiving spirit will always be long-term goals.

International tension

Following Jesus' teaching and example on forgiveness is the key to peace in the modern world. Forgiveness alone can stop the mad cycle of attack and counter-attack which marks so many conflicts. Some of these have the potential to spark World War Three. We are dealing here with life and death issues on a huge scale, not pious platitudes.

It can be made to work. The Truth and Reconciliation Commission pioneered by Desmond Tutu in South Africa has proved this. Because of the power to heal which those painful and emotional gatherings released, this approach has been adopted in other parts of the world, too.

> I think 'forgive us our trespasses' is in some ways one of the most difficult bits of the Lord's Prayer to pray because it reminds us that we're not only saying words, we're expressing a willingness for our lives to be changed.
>
> *Archbishop Rowan Williams*

Forgive us our trespasses as we forgive...

For Jesus the two go together. Our duty to forgive is strongly linked with our own need of forgiveness. He illustrated this in a graphic parable (Matthew 18.23-35).

The New Testament is clear. 'All have sinned and fall short of the glory of God' (Romans 3.23). Each and every one of us desperately needs the forgiveness, grace and generosity of God. Because we have received these vital gifts so freely and abundantly, we are called to spread them around.

Jesus made this uncomfortably plain.

QUESTIONS FOR GROUPS

BIBLE READING: Matthew 5.38-42 & 18.21-22

1. A young teenager is bullied at school and a woman in your street is being abused by her partner. Might you encourage them to forgive? To stand up for themselves? To turn the other cheek? To inform the school/police or to seek other help – and if so, what? Are these options mutually exclusive?

2. *Read Matthew 5.7.* Think of an occasion when you needed to forgive a hurt. And a different occasion when you said sorry to someone you hurt (did they forgive you?). Discuss these situations and perhaps share your own struggles with forgiveness – and what you have learned from them.

3. What do you make of Benoit Witchalls' words (page 16)? Perhaps Julie Nicholson's response is easier to understand? Do you think the Witchalls and Julie Nicholson will feel differently as time passes?

4. 'Forgive us our trespasses...' Some people feel the need for God's forgiveness very keenly, e.g. John Newton in *Amazing Grace* (*'who saved a wretch like me'*). Do you think of yourself as 'a sinner'? Or do you think the Church goes on too much about sin?

5. Re-read the boxes on page 18. Do you agree that a refusal to forgive results in twofold damage – the incident itself and the subsequent bitterness which damages the soul? Is 'refusal' the right word – or should we substitute 'inability'? In contrast, does forgiveness set us free to move on with our lives? Share experiences.

6. Following Ivan Karamazov (page 18) are some crimes/sins too appalling to be forgiven?

7. Desmond Tutu's initiative in setting up the Truth and Reconciliation Commission is often given as an example of good practice. List some of the major conflicts raging in our world right now. Do you agree that forgiveness is the key to long-term solutions? Or is this naive?

8. *Read Matthew 5.44 and Romans 12.14.* What do you make of the distinction between *emotional* forgiveness and *practical* forgiveness (page 18). Is it possible to dislike – or even feel hatred towards – our abusers, yet still to forgive them in a practical sense, i.e. refuse revenge, help them if they are in need (money, letters, food...) and pray for them?

9. What about Michael Saward's approach? Can it be true forgiveness if we want our abusers to receive the full legal punishment? Or is that fatally flawed?

10. Some people are so bruised by life that they feel it is God who needs *their* forgiveness, rather than the other way round. How would you respond if someone said that to you?

You might like to give some thought to Question 9 in Session 5 before your next meeting.

SESSION 5

IN HEAVEN

When Stonebridge people went to the cinema they had to watch the end of the film first, because if they stayed until the finish of the second house, they missed the last bus. (From *The Orchard on Fire*)

This amusing aside from Shena Mackay's novel casts light on the New Testament concept of heaven. St Paul assures us that 'our citizenship is in heaven' (Philippians 3.20). And we are given hints and glimpses of the glory which awaits us. Our main calling is to attend to the early stages of the plot, i.e. our discipleship in *this* world. But as we do this, we already have some idea as to how the whole drama will develop.

Heaven was an important concept for Jesus. His own disciples are to rejoice that their 'names are written in heaven' (Luke 10.20). Heaven erupts in joy when a single sinner repents (Luke 15.7). The phrase 'in heaven' occurs twice in this short pattern prayer. Heaven is the place where God is ('our Father in heaven'); and it is the place where God's will is perfectly performed. ('Thy will be done on earth as it is in heaven'). But perhaps 'place' is the wrong word. Perhaps *anywhere* is heaven, when God's will is being done there?

Certainly Jesus doesn't teach that God is locked away from us in heaven. He is close at hand. Jesus talked to God without a megaphone. He encourages us to do the same.

Ancient and modern

For our forebears life was 'poor, nasty, brutish and short' (Thomas Hobbes, 1588-1679). Death was never far away. So for most of them the concept of heaven was immediate and significant. For similar reasons it is still vitally important in many non-Western cultures today.

Perhaps there are two main reasons why heaven seems to carry less weight for us: our relative longevity and the comfort and security which we enjoy. When death is an ever-present reality, human beings are keenly aware of their own mortality. When life is 'nasty, brutish and short', the notion of a rich exciting life after this one becomes an attractive – even strongly desired – prospect.

Significantly, the modern secular world has not altogether lost this wistfulness in the face of death. David Winter in *The Archbishop's School of Life after Death*[*] makes a telling point (see box).

Central to Christian belief is the notion that none of us can *earn* the abundant life of heaven. If we are to be saved it is by the grace and mercy of God, not by our own

> In conversations with other people who, like myself, have lost a very close partner or a cherished child, I have never met one who answered the question 'Do you believe they no longer exist?' in the affirmative. Most are emphatic that the one they love still exists, even though they can't imagine how or where.
>
> *Canon David Winter*

---

*Available from York Courses – see centre pages of this booklet

> People believe in heaven for various reasons. Near death experiences, for example, or because they can't believe that they will never see their loved ones again ... Christian belief about the reality of heaven is rooted in the strong evidence for Easter. God raised Jesus and death was defeated. God forgives and receives shabby people like you and me. We are all sinners saved by grace.

good deeds. We need forgiveness and – as the Lord's Prayer so strongly indicates – forgiveness is on offer.

In one sense, this seems unfair. Surely a Hitler or an Ian Huntley deserves to be punished for his terrible deeds. Perhaps they will be. But Jesus insists that mercy and forgiveness are always there for the asking. Which is just as well – for which of us does not need the saving grace of God?

If we adopt an atheistic viewpoint, the same apparent unfairness prevails. On this view we all escape from the eternal consequences of our misdeeds – however terrible they may be, and whether or not we are penitent. Like everyone else, we 'escape' into Empty Nothingness. Conversations with atheist friends reveal that they seek, and sometimes gain, comfort from their apparently bleak faith. Non-existence and nothingness mean no more joy. But they also mean no more suffering, no accountability and no consequences of guilt. Some find this attractive.

Pie in the sky?

It is the notion of *comfort* that is often attacked by opponents of Christianity. This attack comes from various angles:

- ❖ Karl Marx famously described religion as 'the opium of the people'. Interestingly, Charles Kingsley – an Anglican cleric and Christian Socialist – used the phrase before Marx. Certainly it was – and perhaps still is – convenient for wealthy and unscrupulous employers/slave or serf owners to point to a glorious future, as compensation for lack of equality and justice in this world. Kingsley showed his keen awareness of these issues in Victorian England, in his novel about chimney-boys, *The Water Babies*.
- ❖ Sigmund Freud took another tack. He argued that Christians have created the father figure we so desperately want. Christian belief in heaven is wishful thinking, according to Freud. Despite his massive influence ('we are all post-Freudians now'), Freud's take on the world has been criticised by many fine minds – not all of them Christian. Sigmund is not necessarily right.

Indeed, the argument based on wishful thinking can be applied equally to atheism. Aldous Huxley, author of *Brave New World*, admitted that for many years he accepted atheism for just this reason. He didn't *want* the world to have any long-term meaning, because he wanted to live without irksome moral controls. Later in life, he was honest enough to admit his motives for believing this.

> The longing for a place where justice is done, where joy lasts, where beauty does not wither, and where peace reigns is a hunger of the human heart, not only of the Christian heart. To dwell on the city where dreams come true is not escapism.
>
> *Revd Dr John Pridmore*

> He who puts us in this life does not abandon His work for any reason or default at the end of it. That is all I have come to learn out of my life. So there is no fear.
>
> *Rudyard Kipling*

Suicide bombers

Like all good things, the notion of heaven can be distorted and misapplied.

I heard (on television) a rabble-rousing preacher from the militant Islamic minority exhorting young men to give their lives as suicide bombers: 'You will not regret it.' How many of those impressionable young people are led down that tragic path by the notion of martyrdom and the promise of heaven?

Of course, most Muslims are as appalled at this distortion of true religion for political ends as Christians are. Recently I met an Imam who, when asked about suicide bombers, asserted that taking innocent life is the road to hell. We understand the dilemma felt by Muslims, for we share it. Believers in Britain were greatly distressed that opposing 'Christian' camps invoked religion during the Troubles in Northern Ireland. We recall that 'the Troubles' was code for bloody violence.

Glory!

But we end on a positive note. It is my conviction that today's Church should speak more about the glories of heaven. Dying, deathbeds and infant mortality were realities for most Victorians. In the West today – unlike most of the world – we are shielded from much of this, for which I am profoundly grateful. But we all encounter death eventually. In the end, each of us must face our own mortality and we need the tools to do this.

The Christian belief in a glorious life 'in heaven' is rooted in the great events we celebrate at Easter. Having studied the evidence for the resurrection of Jesus, I am convinced that God did indeed raise Jesus from the grave. He defeated death and has thrown wide open the gates of glory. The Church worldwide celebrates this wonderful truth at Easter when it declares:

> *Alleluia! Christ is risen.*
> *He is risen indeed. Alleluia!*

> I have a sinne of feare, that when I have spunne/My last thred, I shall perish on the shore;/But sweare by thy selfe, that at my death thy sonne/Shall shine as he shines now, and heretofore;/And, having done that, Thou hast done,/I feare no more.
>
> *John Donne, Dean of St Paul's (1621-31)*

The New Testament gives no basis for widespread concerns about eternal boredom. True, we say 'rest in peace'. But that prayer continues, '… and rise in GLORY'. Jesus pictures heaven as a great party. Perhaps we can best think of it as a place of zest, activity, harmony, friendship and never-ending discovery. Jesus invites us to join the vibrant life of heaven with humility, joy and more than a touch of trepidation. He insists on only one condition – that we come to 'our Father in heaven' with a simple but sincere prayer on our lips. 'Forgive us our trespasses as we forgive those who trespass against us.'

QUESTIONS FOR GROUPS
BIBLE READING: 1 Corinthians 15.12-23

1. It is often asserted that, in contrast to earlier centuries, most Westerners today don't reflect much on their own mortality and what happens after death. Do you think this is true in general? Is it true for you personally? Does it matter?

2. For Religious Education homework, a young person is required to ask several people if they believe in heaven – and if so, why? How would you answer?

3. *Read 1 John 3.1-3.* Some people have an unshakeable faith in heaven and are sure they will be there, by the grace of God. Others oscillate and have doubts (like John Donne – see box on page 23). What about you?

4. Do you believe hell and/or non-existence are realities too – or in your view will everyone go to heaven? Might this be via 'purgatory' – when we are made to face up to our shortcomings and invited to allow God to fill us with his love?

5. What do you feel about the possibility that Adolf Hitler and Ian Huntley might go to heaven? Would you prefer to think of them in hell? Or perhaps that they might simply cease to exist?

6. What might motivate a young suicide bomber? Hatred, certainly. Indoctrination and misplaced loyalty, probably. It seems that the concepts of martyrdom and heaven may also play a large part in this. Can you begin to understand how this works?

7. Some see suicide bombers as villains, while others see them as heroes. Yet others see them as victims. What's your opinion? Try to imagine the thoughts and feelings of a young person trying to decide whether to become a suicide bomber.

8. *Read Revelation 21.1-4.* The famous King's College Carol Service describes those who have already died as being 'on another shore and in a greater light'. Many who've had a near-death experience speak of warmth and light. What do you think heaven might be like – and does this bring you comfort?

9. Choose one hymn and one Bible passage which give you support and encouragement as you contemplate your own mortality.

10. *Read John 20.10-18.* Heaven and Earth meet on Easter Day (page 23). On the CD we asked our participants what Easter means to them and how they like to celebrate it. How would you answer?

11. Re-read and discuss the box at the foot of page 13.

12. Raise any points from the course booklet or CD/audiotape which haven't been covered in any of your discussions but which you find interesting and would like to consider further.

13. You might want to look ahead and discuss possible future plans for your group.

Please pray for all involved with *York Courses* – those who produce the materials and those who use them.